# Kids on the Move

*25 Activities to Help Kids Connect, Reflect & Thrive Around the World*

Leah Evans & Jodi Harris, MSW

# About this Book

If you have this book, you are a third culture kid, someone in the midst of transition, or a person living with change. Whatever your background, wherever you live, whoever you are, this book has activities that will help you learn, grow, and connect. We hope it will also help you see the beauty, the strength, and the adaptability you certainly already possess. Kids on the move often have an ability to see more clearly, understand more deeply, and connect with others in a more significant manner. There are struggles to being transient and living in a place that doesn't feel like home. In this book, we hope you will find ways to deal with those struggles, to process them, and to weave them into the fabric of your identity.

While the activities are organized in a way we think makes sense, you should complete them in a way that works for you. Flip through the book, read the introductions to each activity, and complete them in a way that works for you. This is your book. You can doodle, write comments to yourself or to us; the writers, color, make designs, or whatever you want. Think of it as a journal and a place to share what you are thinking or feeling. If an activity annoys you or doesn't help, you can scribble it out, mark it with a giant X, or change the directions. We invite and encourage you to use the book in a way that makes sense for you.

Mostly, we hope you realize that there are lots of amazing kids just like you out there in this big world. You are amazing. You are adaptable. You are strong.

Enjoy.

# To Parents, Counselors and Teachers

As the parents of third culture children, we know that transitions and living in a place that doesn't feel like home can be challenging. This book was created to provide activities that challenge children to think about their values, their connections, and their place both at home and abroad. The activities are designed to encourage children to see their own resilience, break out of negative patterns, and embrace the unique aspects of a nomadic lifestyle. We aim to promote coping skills that allow children to see their value and the value of their experiences.

The activities can be completed in order or you can skip around and work on those that directly address current challenges. We encourage completing the activities slowly and allowing plenty of time for discussion, reflection, and application. The whole family can benefit from a deeper look at some of the challenges faced by children in a mobile lifestyle.

Throughout the book we have made every effort to include language that represents children of all backgrounds. While this book is written with third culture kids in mind, we recognize that not all children, parents or counselors use or are familiar with that term. However for the sake of clarity, we found there were times when using third culture kid was the best option. We thank you for remembering that this book is really about and for all kids who move…no matter where they're from, where they live or where they're headed.

Children who live abroad, move to new locations, or transition frequently are often strong, adaptable, open-minded, and interesting. We hope this book encourages growth and understanding while undergoing these journeys.

To learn more about us and for contact information, please see the About the Authors section in the back of the book.

Sincerely,

Leah and Jodi

# Disclaimer

For Adults:

We believe these activities are an incredible resource for helping young people connect, reflect and thrive outside their home cultures, during transition and in navigating a globally mobile life. They are meant to be used as a guide and to facilitate thought and discussion. While we thoroughly believe children will find numerous positive benefits from completing the activities, the activities herein should not be used in lieu of professional advice or support. It is recommended and assumed that anyone completing these activities will seek the support of a professional as needed.

For Kids:

If you are struggling, please get help from a grown-up that you trust. Completing these activities is like journaling. It is designed to help you think about what it's like to be a kid on the move, but it is not a substitute for talking about your feelings with a parent, counselor or teacher. Don't be alone. Get help!

# Copyright and Use

All of the content provided here is copyrighted and the property of Leah Evans (After School Plans) and Jodi Harris (World Tree Coaching, LLC). The content here should not be distributed, reproduced or altered without the permission of both authors. Please contact the authors at the contact information provided in the back of the book with any questions or to learn more about how to purchase copies.

## Table of Contents

| | |
|---|---|
| My Dream Suitcase | 8 |
| Bad Day Permission Slip | 9 |
| My Favorite Things | 10 |
| Build a Bridge | 12 |
| An Illustrated Adventure | 13 |
| The Fortune Teller | 15 |
| Problem Solving | 18 |
| Get Curious | 20 |
| Family Tree | 22 |
| Family Tree Part II | 24 |
| My Tribe | 27 |
| Mantra | 28 |
| Where I Wear My Emotions | 31 |
| Finding Stillness | 33 |
| Building Resilience | 35 |
| Giving Back | 36 |
| Keeping an Open Mind | 37 |
| Goal Collage | 39 |
| My Favorite Dinner Party | 41 |
| Staying in Touch | 42 |
| Look Ahead | 44 |
| My Timeline So Far | 45 |
| My Potential Future Timeline | 46 |
| Siblings, With Us All the Way | 47 |
| Who Am I? | 49 |
| Where Are You From | 50 |
| Where on Earth Have I Been | 52 |

# Activities

## My Dream Suitcase

Moving means a lot of goodbyes. Do you ever wish you could just take everything you love with you? Everything that's important, everything that you miss so much when you leave?

Sometimes it helps to imagine being able to do that. We can't change the fact that some things, people and places must be left behind, but when we take time to think about taking those things with us, it makes it easier to think about how we remember them when they're far away.

In the space below, fill your suitcase with everything you'd take with you if you could. You can use drawings, words, magazine clippings, anything...

## Bad Day Permission Slip

Let's face it, some days are really bad. Despite all of the adventures you may be having, your life is a lot like everyone else's – there are up days and down days.

Sometimes we lead ourselves to believe that it's not okay to have a bad day. We're convinced there's something wrong with us or that we're just complaining. But having bad days is normal and the main thing we can do on those days is to take care of ourselves. This activity gives you permission to do just that.

Please remember - if your bad days start to outnumber your good days – it's time to get some help. Please ask a trusted friend, teacher or family member for support.

To Whom It May Concern:

(                              ) is having a bad day. It's just one of those days. You know how it goes. We all have them. Therefore today, in order to take care of her/himself, she/he will:

## My Favorite Things

When you move around a lot it can be difficult to remember all of your favorite things. You get a collection of little odds and ends from all over. Sometimes these are actual things, but many times, the items you've collected are memories of places or moments that have had an impact on your life. These all make up your favorite things (even if some of them weren't all that great!). In the spaces below – think of some of your favorite things you've acquired, seen, experienced, or come to know in your journey. Remember – this doesn't have to be just "things."

Something old:

Something new:

Something brightly colored:

Something without much color:

Something sad:

Something happy:

Something quiet:

Something loud:

Something that smells nice:

Something that smells bad:

Something that you loved:

Something that you hated:

Something that you can carry in your pocket:

Something that you need a suitcase for:

Something that you learned from:

Something that felt like a waste of time:

Something you did on your own:

Something you did with friends or family:

## Build a Bridge

Living in a place far from what you consider to be home can sometimes make you feel cut off from your home culture. Sometimes going home after living abroad makes you feel like you don't fit in anywhere. Consider yourself as a bridge, bringing together two different cultures, sharing them with others, and expanding your personal space with rich and varied experiences, friends, and understandings. In this activity, draw or write the things that you appreciate about the home you just left and the home where you are living now, one on each side of the bridge. Then, draw a picture of yourself in the middle of the bridge.

Reflection: How has your knowledge of two or more different cultures increased your understanding of people and places?

_____
_____
_____
_____

## An Illustrated Adventure

That time right before we head out on another adventure can feel like the place of our wildest imaginations. Our dreams become more vivid and our mind-wandering moments are filled with both excitement and dread as we think about where we're headed next and the unknowns that are laid out before us.

Allowing ourselves to fully picture that story can be a great way to make sense of what we *know* to be true, what we *believe* to be true (but can't really prove) and what probably *isn't* true, but makes us feel scared or worried.

In this activity, you're invited to create a comic strip of your journey. You can use yourself as the protagonist or a fictional character. You can make it realistic or it can be a safe place to convey your fears or doubts. Include your wildest dreams of fun and adventure or the everyday moments that you expect to encounter. Allow yourself to be creative. More boxes are continued on the next page.

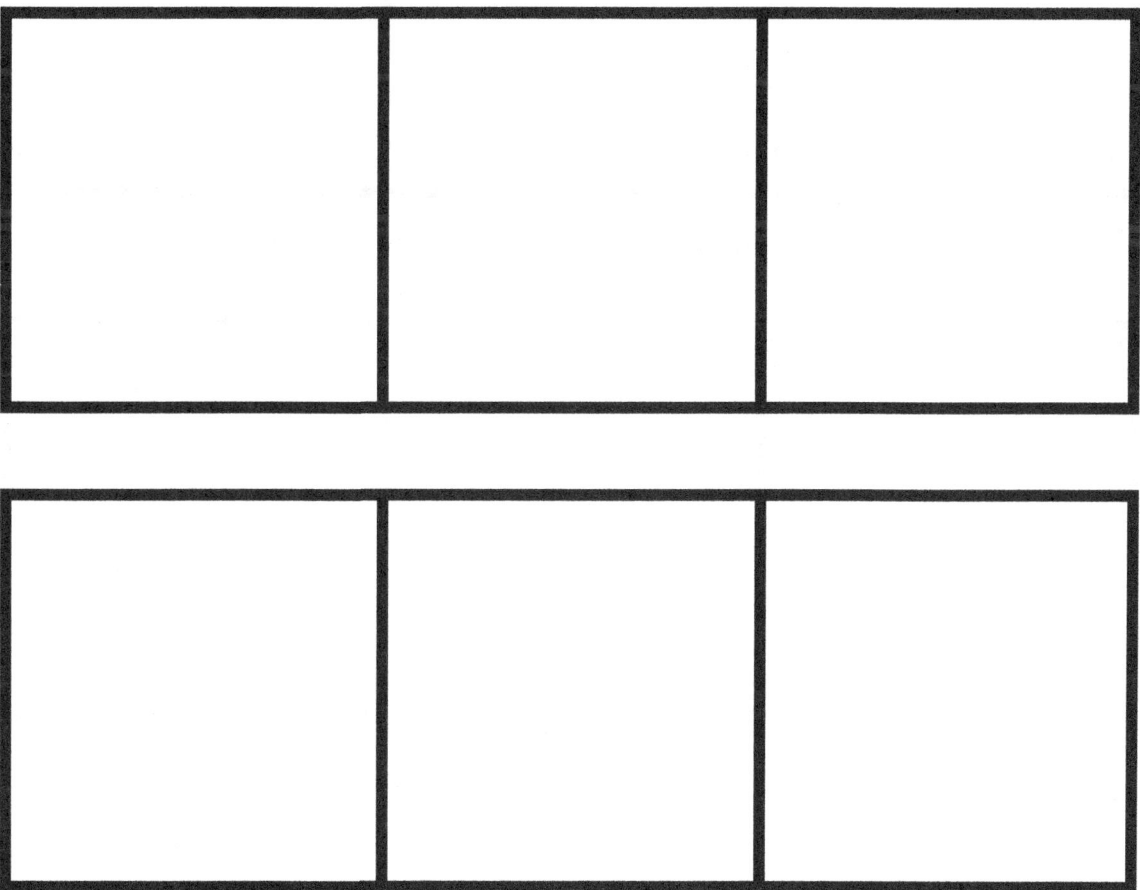

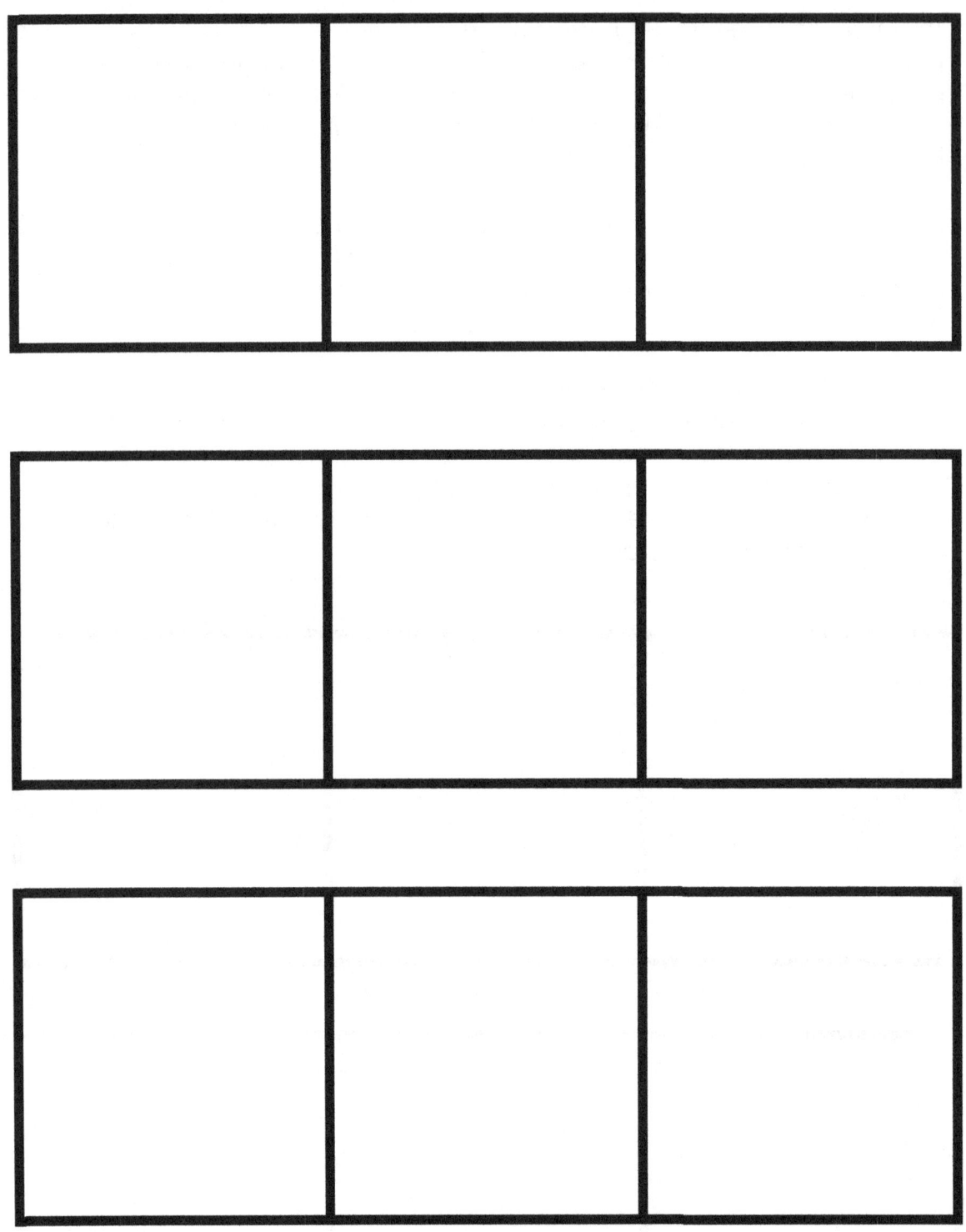

# The Fortune-Teller

Sometimes it would be nice to have a fortune-teller who could reassure us that the future will turn out okay. Of course, it's impossible...but it's always nice to dream. One of the biggest challenges humans face with regard to the future is that it's all in our heads. There is literally nowhere to go because we simply cannot predict what's going to happen. The result is that we get stuck in a loop of trying to guess what will happen. And that gets exhausting! It's like running in circles.

So how do we get out of that loop? One way is to remove those predictions from our head so that we can acknowledge them. Additionally, we benefit from giving our mind the space it needs to see how likely this perceived future is to occur. That's what you're going to do here.

In the spaces below, list one of your predictions about the future. There is space for 5, but feel free to add more in a journal or on a separate piece of paper. Don't worry if the event seems really unlikely – if you're thinking about it, it matters and for this exercise it's worth your time!

Then, rate the likelihood of the event on the scale from 1-10.

1= Almost impossible. Highly UNLIKELY to happen.

10 = This will happen. Almost (or absolutely) 100% chance.

The goal with this exercise is to give you the chance to see where you can take action and where you can set aside your worries.

For example, if you're a nervous flyer and you're moving overseas, well there is a 100% chance that you will have to fly. This helps you plan for how you will prepare for that stressor. What about if you're thinking you'll never see your boyfriend or girlfriend again? Perhaps that falls into the lower end of the scale – around a 2, perhaps? This frees you up to plan for how you'll keep in touch, what steps you want to take to maintain the relationship and make decisions about how you'll move forward.

In other words, you get the chance to release the worry and take action.

1.
_____
_____
_____
_____
_____
_____
_____
_____
_____
_____

SCALE:

1.......2.......3.......4.......5.......6.......7.......8.......9.......10

2.
_____
_____
_____
_____
_____
_____
_____
_____
_____
_____

SCALE:

1.......2.......3.......4.......5.......6.......7.......8.......9.......10

3.
_____
_____
_____
_____
_____
_____
_____
_____
_____
_____

SCALE:

1.......2.......3.......4.......5.......6.......7.......8.......9.......10

4.

_____
_____
_____
_____
_____
_____
_____
_____
_____

SCALE:

1.......2.......3.......4.......5.......6.......7.......8.......9.......10

5.

_____
_____
_____
_____
_____
_____
_____
_____
_____

SCALE:

1.......2.......3.......4.......5.......6.......7.......8.......9.......10

6.

_____
_____
_____
_____
_____
_____
_____
_____
_____

SCALE:

1.......2.......3.......4.......5.......6.......7.......8.......9.......10

## Problem Solving

Sometimes things aren't really working the way we want them to. It's easy to complain or give up, but here we want to help you think of ways to solve the problem you may be facing. Maybe you already do this, but it's still helpful to work through specific steps for some of those more challenging issues that defy solutions. How do you do that?

1. State the problem. (Make this as short and simple as you can!)
2. Explain the factors or contributing issues. (What causes the problem?)
3. Offer a solution. (This is your preferred solution.)
4. Offer alternative solutions. (What other solutions would be acceptable to you?)
5. Compromise.

Here is a sample of a script you can solve yourself:

1. The problem is that I am getting a bad grade in math.
2. The contributing issue is that I am not doing my homework.
3. My solution is that I will do my homework after dinner every night.
4. Alternatively, I will ask to stay after school for homework club every day.
5. I will compromise by doing homework at home some nights and after school some days.

Here is an example of a problem you could solve with your parents:

1. The problem is that I am not happy in my current school.
2. A factor is that I love to do art and this school is science based.
3. My solution is that I would like to change schools to an art school.
4. If that doesn't work, I would like to take art classes after school.
5. I will compromise and take an online drawing class that is offered for free.

This way, your parents know your concerns, know what causes them, and can help you figure out a solution. You might want to try this script if you want to start a new activity, quit an activity, find new friends, move home, or change your room around. You can use the script for just about anything! Of course, having a problem-solving strategy doesn't mean you will solve the problem, or solve it in the way you want, but it is always worth a try! Let's go through the steps for a problem you have right now!

## Think of something that is bothering you and write out a script.

Dear Mom, Dad, Teacher, Counselor, or Sibling, I would like to talk to you about:
_____
_____
_____

State Problem:
_____
_____
_____

Contributing Factors:
_____
_____
_____

Solution:
_____
_____
_____

Alternative Solution:
_____
_____
_____

Compromise:
_____
_____
_____

## Get Curious!

In this lifestyle – the phrase "curiosity killed the cat," is definitely not true! We have to be curious if we're to make the very best of a world that is so full of things that we don't understand. Curiosity is the fuel of international kids.

You've got so many questions – boring ones, simple ones, super smart ones, extremely difficult ones, ones that may not even have answers.

Some of your questions are about your move. Others are about what comes next for you. And still others are about what life will be like in the next phase (whether you're moving again or staying put).

Sometimes it can help us to get some answers. Other times we simply have to recognize that the question we're asking may not really have an answer that we can know ahead of time...and that's okay. But, either way, putting our questions down on paper can be a huge step towards organizing our thoughts and feeling so that we feel like we have a bit more control. Committing to finding answers gives us something to focus on. Recognizing that the answers may not exist enables us to accept and move on when we need to.

In this exercise, you'll list your questions – all of them, some of them or simply the most pressing right now. In the check boxes to the right, place a check when you have your answer. And here's the important thing about the answer – it's when you have the answer that works best for you! That means – when you feel satisfied that you're where you want to be with that particular question.

| Question | Answered |
|---|---|
|  |  |
|  |  |
|  |  |

|  |  |
|---|---|
|  |  |
|  |  |
|  |  |
|  |  |
|  |  |
|  |  |
|  |  |
|  |  |
|  |  |
|  |  |
|  |  |
|  |  |

## Family Tree Activity

What do you know about your ancestors? People often trace their family history using a family tree. This is because we flourish and grow and expand thanks to the roots set by those who came before us. It's important to remember our connection to our family and those roots as we set out into the world and grow in different places.

In this activity, we ask you to put the living members of your family in the section of the tree with the leaves. Write their name, birthdate, and connection to you (mother, father, grandmother, aunts, etc.) Also, write the name of the city where they live. Around the roots include as many family members as you can uncover that are no longer living. Include grandparents, great-grandparents, great-aunts, second cousins and anyone else that are a part of your foundation. Include their birth and death dates and where they lived (for most of the time). You will probably need a parent to help you with this activity!

While adding your ancestors, ask questions about what they were like, where they lived, and what challenges they faced.

Some people don't know that much about their family history, and that's okay. If you can't find information about family members, complete the tree as an imaginative tree of wishes. Who would you like to be related to? Add in kings, queens, world leaders, famous people, or even fictional characters. Next to each person you add, write down one characteristic or description that explains your connection. You might use words like "brave," "strong," "adventurous," "smart," or "athletic." You get to choose!

## Family Tree Part II

Next, interview some of your living family members to learn some more about three of the ancestors you included on the tree. Use the following five questions to guide you but feel free to add more. If you don't have access to information about relatives, it's okay to include an important friend.

**Relative One**

Name:

Relationship to you:

Date and Place of Birth:

Date and Place of Death:

Describe the person:

What was one hardship that this person faced?

How did they overcome that hardship?

**Relative Two**

Name:

Relationship to you:

Date and Place of Birth:

Date and Place of Death:

Describe the person:

What was one hardship that this person faced?

How did they overcome that hardship?

**Relative Three**

Name:

Relationship to you:

Date and Place of Birth:

Date and Place of Death:

Describe the person:

What was one hardship that this person faced?

How did they overcome that hardship?

## My Tribe

Moving around a lot can make you feel incredibly independent. You're amazing in airports and foreign supermarkets. You've mastered the loud and crazy street bazaars and the ins and outs of greetings.

And yet, we all have those moments when we need a hand, an ear or an embrace. We all need that. It's not a sign of weakness or evidence of a problem when we have to ask for help. It's a sign of strength. It can be helpful to plan ahead. When we're feeling stressed or alone, that can be the most difficult time to think off the tops of our heads. In this exercise, you can do a bit of planning ahead.

Think about your tribe – the people who know you, support you and love you no matter what. This is about the people who want to come to your side when you're struggling. These people will drop everything to be there for you. Use the boxes below to identify some of these important people in your life – the ones you'll reach out to when the going gets tough.

| Family | Friends |
|---|---|
| | |

| Teachers/Helpers | Community Members |
|---|---|
| | |

## Mantra

Imagine you're faced with a difficult choice, a challenging situation or a stressful conversation. How do you say or do the right thing? How do you know what's right for you? What skills will you use to filter out your voice from the voice of so many others?

We all benefit from having a set of words to live by. Of course, those words can change over time as we learn new things, meet new people, and grow into ourselves. But, learning how to create your personal mantra is a skill you can take with you wherever you go. That's what we're going to do in this exercise.

In this space list 5 people that you most admire (this can be people you know personally or people you don't know personally):

Now, list the personal characteristics that you most value in these people (i.e. What is it about them that makes them admirable?):

Here, list what you most admire about yourself:

[ ]

Look at the two lists of personal characteristics above, list the 10 that you feel are the most important for your own life (this can include ones from your list about yourself or ones that you aspire to because you've witnessed them in others):

[ ]

Now here's the hard part – cut that list down to 5:

[ ]

These 5 personality traits constitute your personal vision or mantra for how you want to engage with the world. For example, let's say you chose Loving, Fun, Kind, Curious and Persistent. When faced with a difficult situation you can ask yourself if you're remembering these words in the choices you're making.

Concerned that you'll have trouble remembering? Here are a couple ideas for how to make these words memorable:

1. Create an art piece that includes the words.
2. Make an Instagram post for each word (you can even print them out).
3. Make an image you can use as social media header.
4. Print them on a card and frame them, then put them somewhere you see each day.
5. Other ideas? Do some brainstorming below and then choose the option that words best for you.

## Where I Wear My Emotions

If you've ever felt nervous (we all have!), it's easy to know exactly where nervousness shows up in your body. It's often right there in the butterfly-filled pit of your stomach, in the sweaty palm of your hands or in the rapid thumping of your heart.

That can be a pretty easy one, but with other emotions – we don't always pay attention to where we feel them. However, doing so can be a huge step towards learning more about how we feel.

Why? When we notice where emotions show up in our bodies, we notice the little changes that we make to accommodate them. Also, our bodies are incredible predictors of the ways we feel. So, even when we don't "feel" sad or angry or worried, our bodies are often giving us little clues. And those little clues can help us pay attention when and where we need to.

This exercise will help you better understand how emotions show up in your body. On the images below, start by writing the name of the emotion above the picture. Then, write words or color in sections to show how each emotion shows up for you. There are more spaces on the next page.

## Finding Stillness

One of the best things we can offer ourselves is space away from the constant mental, physical and emotional hustle that comes from a life lived all over the world. It can be challenging sometimes to find ways to calm our minds and bodies, but it's a necessary and important step to finding a sense of ease during challenging times.

The cool thing about finding stillness and calming the mind is that you don't actually have to be "still" to practice it. Common activities that can still your mind include - playing sports, running, yoga, knitting, cooking, coloring in a coloring book, dancing, going for a long walk – and so much more.

A cool way to think of it is like the glitter in a snow globe. When you shake it up – that's what your brain might feel like when you're stressed or you've got a lot on your mind. When you stop shaking it, the glitter is still there (our thoughts and troubles don't automatically go away), but when we can find stillness in our mind (even if we're moving our bodies) – we see more clearly and feel a greater sense of balance.

In the space below, take some time to brainstorm and think about the ways in which you find stillness.

I find stillness in _____.

When I do this I notice that I feel:




I find stillness in _____.

When I do this I notice that I feel:

I find stillness in _____.

When I do this I notice that I feel:




I find stillness in _____.

When I do this I notice that I feel:




I find stillness in _____.

When I do this I notice that I feel:

## Building Resilience

Sometimes when we are moving from place to place we feel very fragile and forget that we are actually very strong. As we face obstacles and challenges, it can help to look back and remember times when we were resilient and managed to get through to the other side of a challenging situation. Let's think of three times you were resilient. It could be when you had to start in a new school, when you lost someone or something close to you, when you studied hard and did well in a test, or where you worked hard to reach a goal. In each of the three balls below, write a brief description of a time when you were resilient or you bounced back from a challenge!

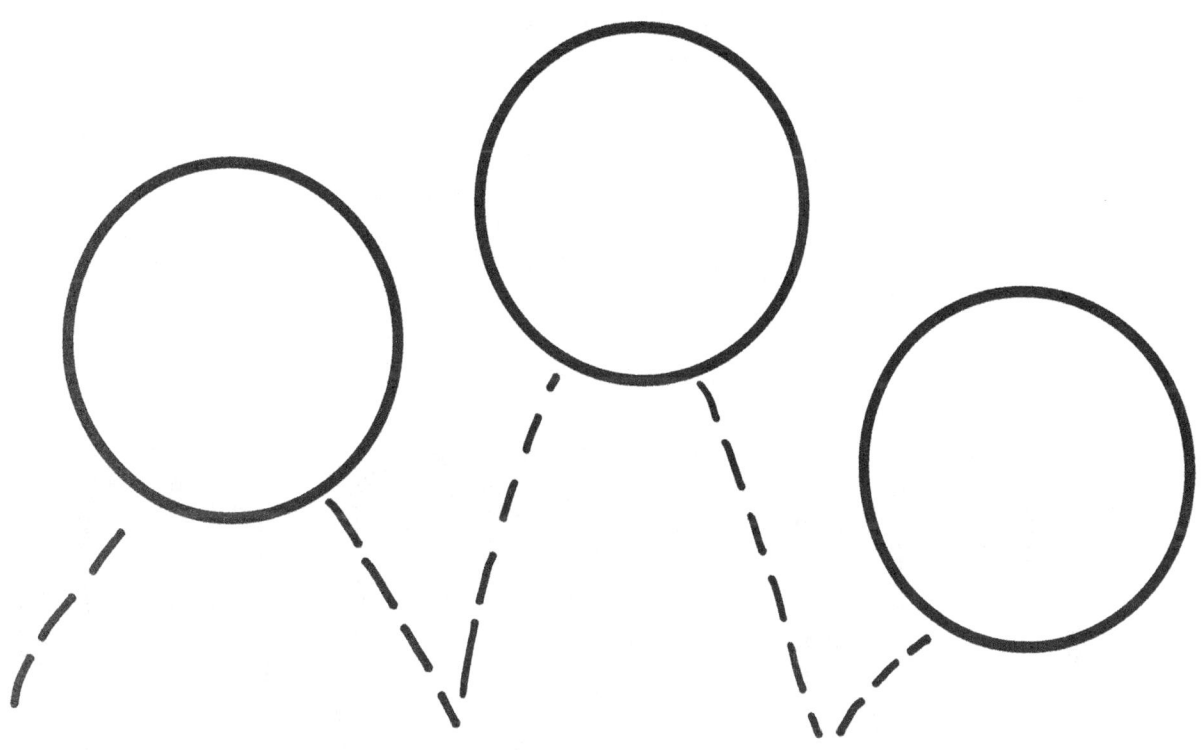

Then, let's look at your three examples and write a quick sentence describing YOU!

I am strong and resilient because I: _____

_____

_____

## Giving Back

Do you find ways to help others? Giving back is a great way to help others and to make a difference in your world. Volunteering is a great way to make friends, learn about a community, and improve the way you feel about life. Maybe you already have a way to volunteer, contribute, or support others. If not, here are a few suggestions:

- Organize a trash pick-up or do one yourself.
- Volunteer at an orphanage.
- Arrange a clothes drive with your friends or family and give to charity.
- Collect gifts for Christmas or equivalent giving holidays for those in need.
- Ask friends and family to give you sample bottles from their hotel visits and then donate them to shelters.
- Walk dogs at an animal shelter.
- Adopt a street pet.

Fill in each hand with a quick idea about how you already are giving to your community or ideas of what you could do in the future. Then, discuss your ideas with a parent.

I would like to give back to my community by:
_____
_____
_____

## Keeping an Open Mind

From the minute we're born, we start to learn things. We learn what's safe and what isn't. We learn what we like and what we don't. And we learn what makes sense and what seems confusing. We learn all of these things from our own personal point of view and experience.

As we move around the world we see this first hand! Many times what we witness around us seems really different from what we've always viewed as normal, right, or acceptable.

So how do we make room for these differences? How do we accept the things that are different while maintaining our own sense of self, culture and identity? In other words – how do we keep an open mind?

The first way we do that is by recognizing the customs, habits, traditions and norms of our own culture. What are some of the things you know to be typical of your home culture, your family or the place you most connect to? Write them in the space below:

_____
_____
_____
_____
_____

Now, think back to a time when you encountered a custom, habit, tradition or norm that seemed really strange to you. What happened? Where were you? Set the scene:

_____
_____
_____
_____
_____

How did you feel when you experienced this difference? What emotions can you remember having?

_____
_____
_____
_____
_____

Now, what thoughts were running through your head? Be honest here! It's okay if you thought what you witnessed was really strange.

_____
_____
_____
_____
_____

Was there anything that was familiar in the situation? What way did the person or group of people seem like you? Was there anything you could relate to even though it was a little different than what you're used to?

_____
_____
_____
_____
_____

What decision did you make about how to handle the different situation? Were you happy with that situation? If so, why? If not, what would you do differently next time?

_____
_____
_____
_____
_____

What did you most learn from this situation? How can you apply that learning to future scenarios?

_____
_____
_____
_____
_____

For many of us, these "culture shock" moments happen frequently. It's common to experience this as we move around. The best way to keep an open mind is to put yourself into reflection mode. Asking these questions reminds us that we have similarities and differences with the different people we encounter – and that's okay! The most important thing is to take time to reflect, to recognize what you can learn and to make a plan for how to maintain an open mind again and again.

## Goal Collage

When you are a kid, sometimes people ask you what you want to be when you grow up. That is certainly a goal but we like to think of our goals more generally. How do you want to feel? What do you want to learn? Who do you want to be? This leaves us with a more general sense of our direction and leaves us more open to adapting and changing our identity as we grow and change.

Here, you can think about some of your goals. Think about the three questions posed above and then draw or cut out pictures that describe the answers. Use your pictures to create a "Goal Collage". You might have a picture of someone winning a game, a photo of a beautiful spot where you might want to live, words that inspire you, or people doing things that interest you. You can find pictures in your photo albums, online, in magazines, or you can draw them yourself.

Use the area below to write down ideas about what you might want to include in your collage. Then, use the next page to make your collage.

## My Favorite Dinner Party

One of the hardest things about going from place to place is the feeling that you're losing important people in your life. Keeping in touch with the people you love when you're moving away takes time and planning. The first step for planning how to keep in touch is to think about the people who've become important to you and why they mean so much. Place your friends' names around the imaginary table below. Imagine yourself sitting down to a meal with these friends and family members. On the table in front of each person, write a couple of words that describe why that person is important to you.

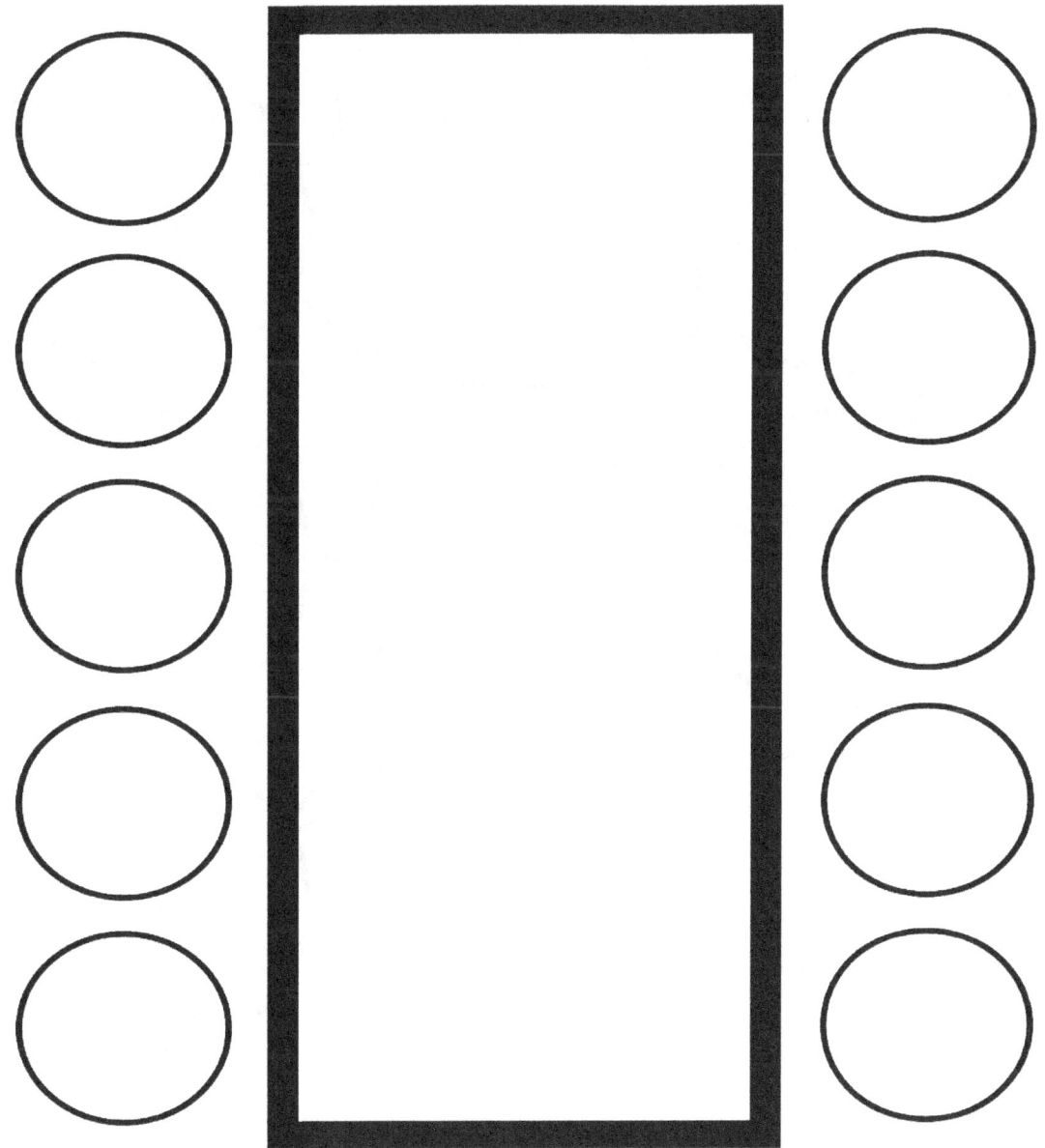

**Staying in Touch**

The next step in figuring out how we will maintain relationships after a move is to make a plan for how to do that. In the diagram below, fill in the middle circle with your name and the other circles with the names of some of your favorite people (for example, from the previous activity – My Favorite Dinner Party). Include their address, email address and phone numbers. Add more circles if you need to! Flip to the next page for some extra connection suggestions.

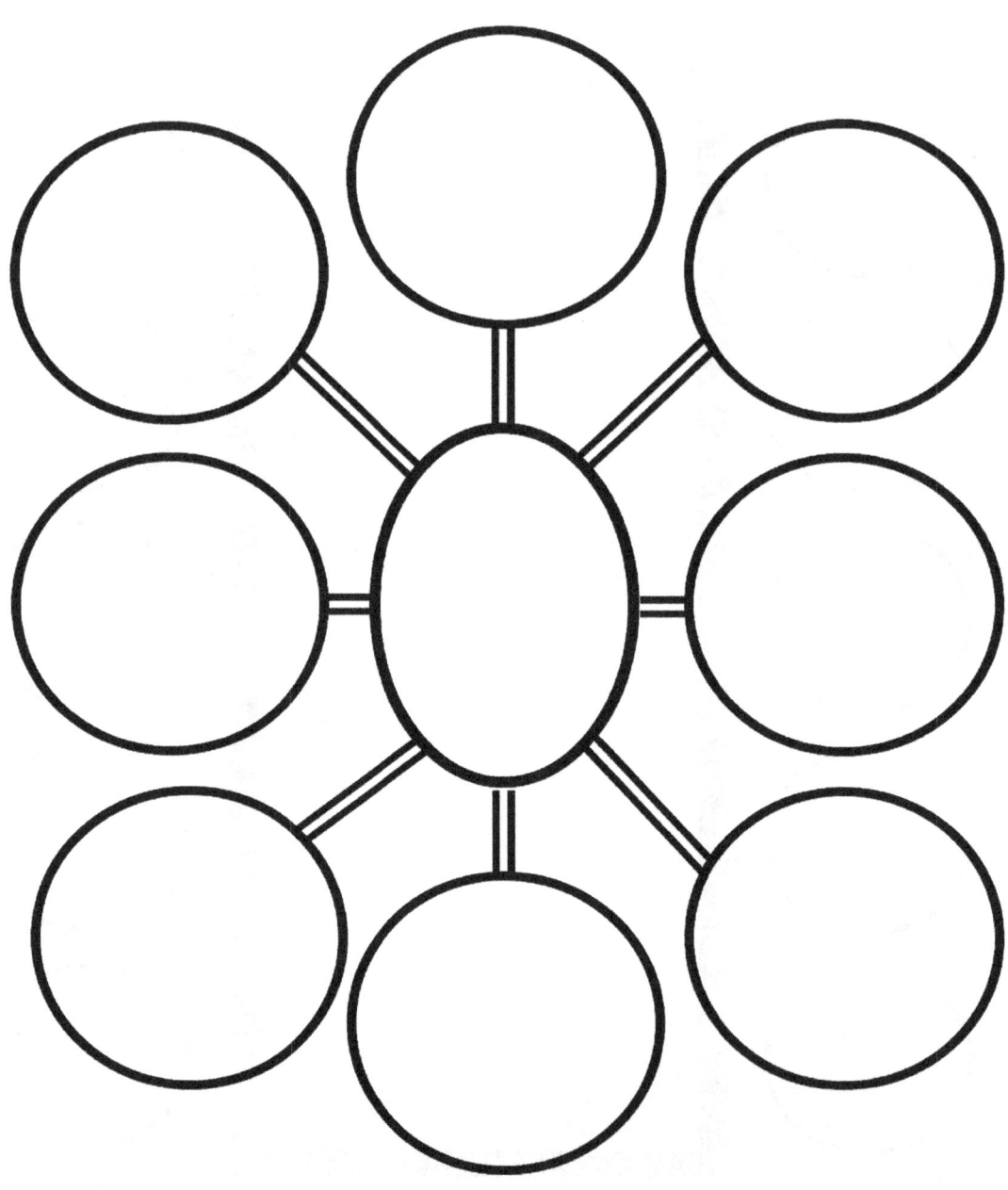

# Connection Suggestions

- Send a small souvenir from your country.
- Start a circle journal. Buy a small journal and each month write one page and paste in two or three pictures. Send to your friend so they can do the same thing and send it back to you.
- Skype or use another way to call your friend online once a month.
- Agree to watch a movie the same week and then discuss it on the phone.
- Start a book club together. Read the same book and then discuss it.
- Pick a topic you know nothing about to learn and then discuss what you learned on the phone or online.

## Look Ahead – Fun Events Coming Up!

If you are new to a place and lonely, bad days can seem endless. It helps to sometimes look ahead and see what's coming and what you can look forward to. Create your own yearly calendar where you list some of your highlights for each month. You can include holidays, family trips, birthdays, seasons, and important school dates. Try to find one positive event for each month. If there isn't one, see if a parent will plan one for you. You might ask for a dinner out, a trip to a park, movie night, or something like "cake day!"

| January | February | March | April |
|---|---|---|---|
| May | June | July | August |
| September | October | November | December |

### Research some of our favorites holidays to add to your calendar!

March 14 - *National Pi Day*: Pi Day is an annual celebration of the mathematical constant π (pi).

April 10 - *National Siblings Day*: Do something kind for your siblings.

April 11 - *National Pet Day*: Walk dogs at your local shelter or shower your own pet with treats!

## My Timeline So Far

When thinking about "me" it can help to create a personal timeline. What are the key events that have happened so far in your life? This activity has two parts. First, you will create your "past" timeline and then you will dream about your "future" timeline. This gives you a sense of where you were and where you want to go. Of course, you never know what will happen so your future timeline will change as you change or as circumstances change. But, it can give you a sense of direction or a sense of where you would like to go. For this part, write down the key events that have happened so far in your life. If you prefer, you can draw pictures or paste photos for an abbreviated timeline of your life. Remember, these are key events that are important to you.

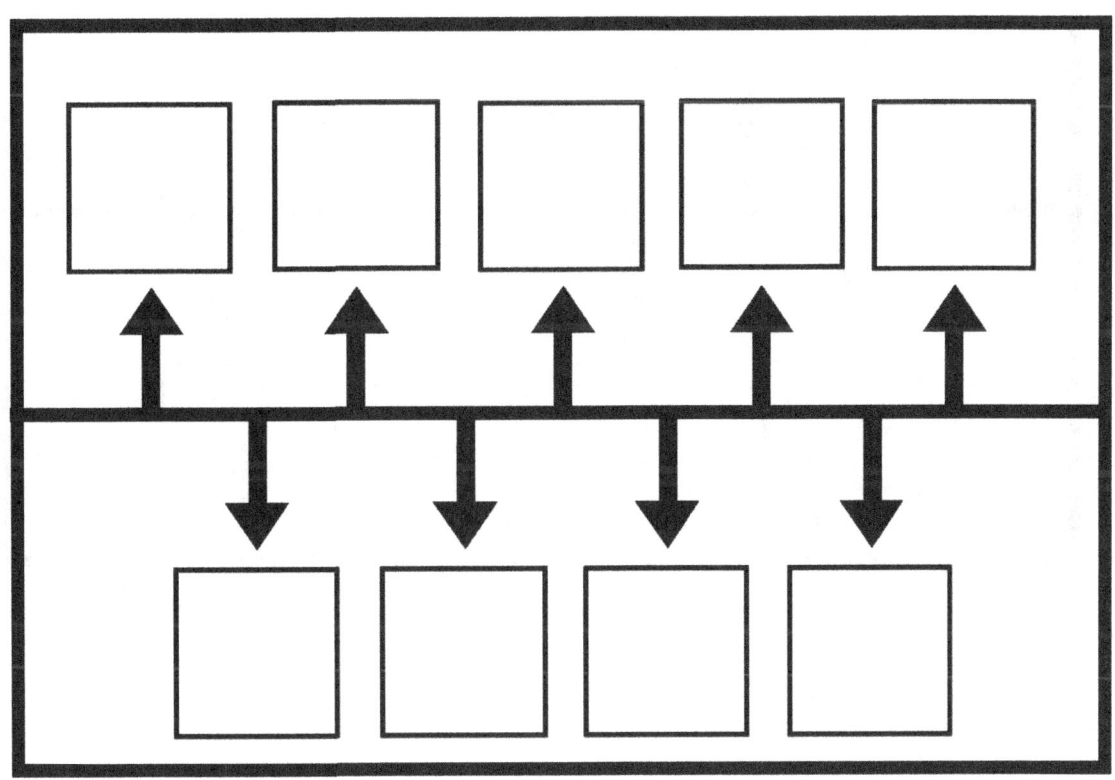

Now, in one to three sentences, pretend to explain your timeline to someone you just met. Example: I was born in Tennessee, moved to Europe where I attended school, started to ride horses, and began to love art. I now live in Ireland.

_____
_____
_____

## My Potential Future Timeline

Now you get to use your imagination! Think of a few milestones you might pass including schooling, relationships, where you might live, and accomplishments you hope to have. Include them in a timeline of your future life!

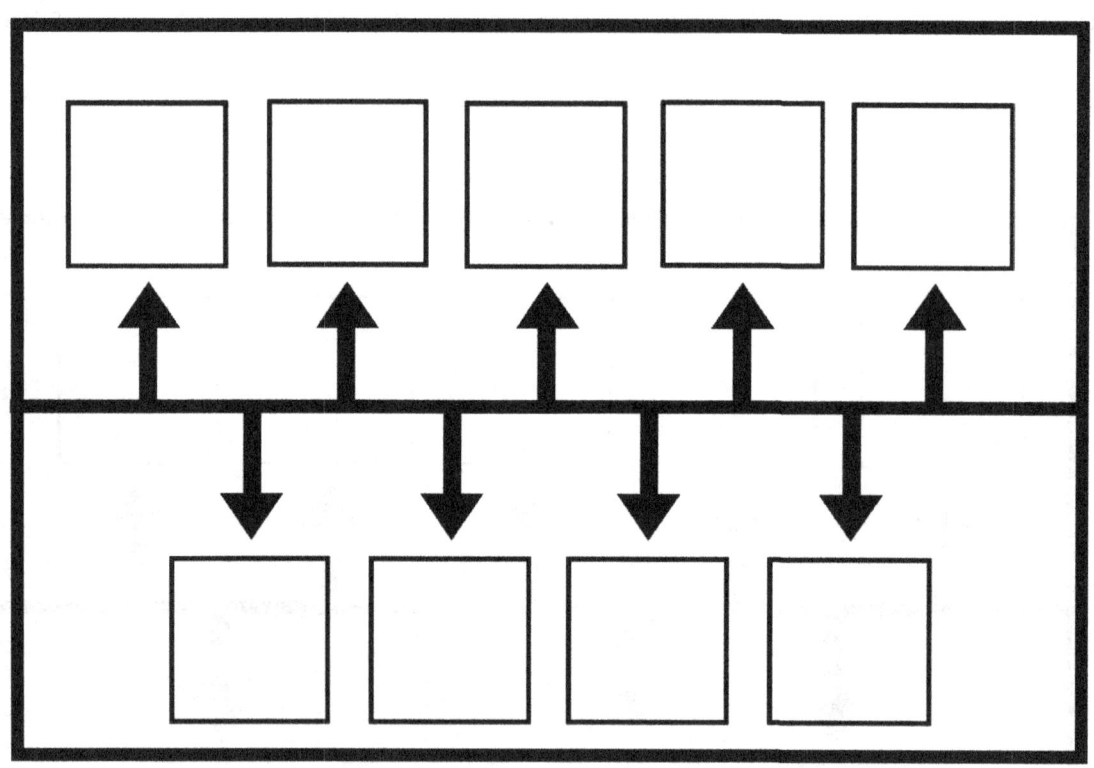

Now, in one to three sentences, pretend to explain your future timeline to someone you just met. Example: I hope to join the debate team in high school and graduate with honors. I want to go to college in the United States and study history. After college I would love to live with my friends in a big city and teach high school.

_____
_____
_____
_____
_____
_____

## Siblings, With Us All the Way!

If you have siblings, you know that they have to go through all of the same challenges that you do as a third culture kid. It's worth thinking about how you can support each other in this unique lifestyle. While siblings don't always get along, they can make a tremendous difference in finding meaning and stability in a transient lifestyle. What can you do to support your siblings?

**LISTEN:** Listen by asking them how they are feeling and doing and then really paying attention to their answer.

**EMPATHIZE**: Empathize by saying that you understand without giving advice or negative feedback.

**SUPPORT**: Support by asking how you can help, sharing your own experiences, and showing them that you are looking out for them.

Now, let's brainstorm! Using the peace sign image on the next page, in each part of the pie, list ways you can listen, empathize, and support your siblings.

(Either paste a picture of your siblings below, or draw a picture of you all together!)

## Who Am I? Create a Word Map

Kids who move around a lot sometimes struggle with describing themselves. This is often because they have had so many profound and important experiences that it's hard to figure out how they all come together into one person! We call this beautiful complexity. The good news is, kids can embrace this and create their own sense of identity by pulling together their diverse experiences and ideas into one coherent, and fascinating, person.

In the graphic below, create a word map with words or short phrases that describe you. Put your name in the center circle. In the outside circles, list languages, countries visited or lived in, adjectives that describe you, relationships, dreams, wishes, strengths, and weaknesses. You can add additional bubbles as needed.

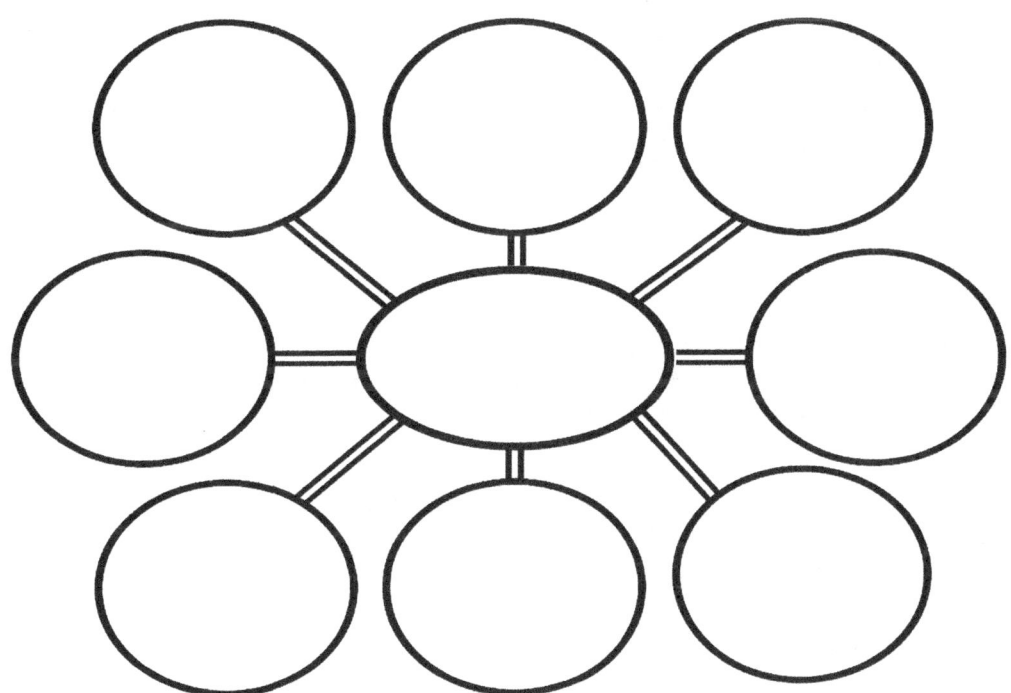

In the space below, use your word map to write a one-sentence description of you. For example: I am a traveler who speaks three languages, loves to find new restaurants, dreams of being an artist, and has played baseball on three continents.

_____
_____
_____

## Where Are You From?

Sometimes third culture kids have a tough time answering the most basic question asked when getting to know someone new. *Where are you from?* It helps to have a prepared answer and to have an idea about how to direct the conversation from there.

### 3 Tips That Might Help

1. Keep it short.
2. Keep it simple.
3. Answer and then ask your own question.

### 1. Keep It Short

*Where are you from?* That's really the hardest question, isn't it? Many times, the questioner wants to know where your family came from originally, or where you have most of your ancestors. You don't have to answer that specific question, though, and you can decide which question you really want to answer. For instance, you can use any of these answers:

I was born in…
I have mostly lived in…
I identify home as……because…(that is where my family is from, that is the place I love the most, that is the place that feels like home, etc.)

### 2. Keep It Simple

You might even try using a formula like:

My passport/family is from _____ but _____ feels like home because _____.

My mom is from _____ and my dad is from _____ but I call _____ home because _____.

For me, home is _____ because _____.

## 3. Answer and Ask Your Own Question

When you're getting to know someone, remember to ask lots of questions! Answer the questions they ask of you, and then ask them questions and really listen to the answers. Make a list of questions that you would like to ask new people you meet. Here are some for inspiration. What questions would you add to this list?

- What place do you call home?
- How long have you lived here?
- What is your favorite thing about living here?
- Tell me something about this country.
- Tell me something about you.
- What are your hobbies?
- What is your favorite restaurant?
- If you could live anywhere, where would it be and why?
- What is your favorite book?
- What is your favorite subject in school?

### Practice, Practice, Practice!

Now, you try it! Use the space below to write your own answer to "Where are you from?". Practice with a friend until it rolls off your tongue. Ask your friend questions about their own life to get the conversation moving.

_____

_____

_____

_____

_____

# Where on Earth Have I Been?

The average American visits three countries in their lifetime and 1/3 of all Americans will never leave the United States. How about you? List all of the countries you have visited, and for fun, color them in on the map.

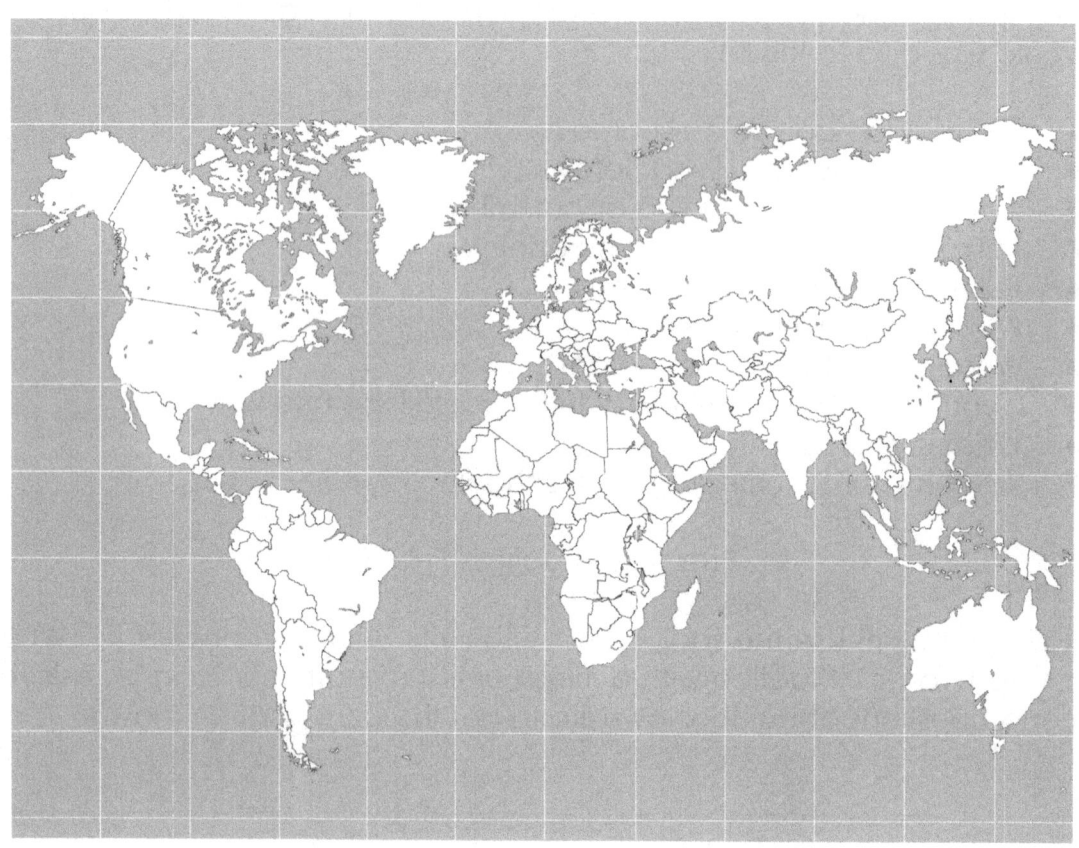

List the countries you have visited below:

_____

_____

_____

List the countries you would like to visit in the future:

_____

_____

_____

# About the Authors

## Leah Moorefield Evans

Leah Moorefield Evans has lived abroad with her Foreign Service husband and four third culture kids since 2005. Her family has lived in Georgia, Ecuador, Ukraine, Paraguay, and Mexico. In 2012, Leah started After School Plans, a website providing relocation resources and American history courses for expat children. A former U.S. History teacher, she created history courses for children through American-History-in-a-Box, full of books, games, and activities so children can learn about the major concepts from their history. She has also published "Kids on the Move, a Relocation Workbook," "The Embassy Kids Coloring Book," and "Patches, the Moving Bear." She edited and collaborated on "Raising Kids in the Foreign Service" with the Associates of the American Foreign Service Worldwide (AAFSW) and "A Cup of Culture and a Pinch of Crisis" with Tales from a Small Planet. She is also a yoga teacher and an artist. Contact Leah by emailing afterschoolplans@gmail.com or by visiting her website at www.afterschoolplans.com.

## Jodi Harris, MSW

Originally from Austin, Texas, Jodi has lived (as of this writing) in Spain, Northern Ireland, the Dominican Republic, Madagascar and Japan. She is raising three third culture kids in loving, if not occasionally chaotic partnership with her husband, a US diplomat. She is a trained clinical social worker, teacher, certified coach (ICF – ACC), writer, T1D mom and the owner of World Tree Coaching, LLC where she offers individual coaching, group coaching and programs in mindfulness and Personal Leadership to individuals living outside their home cultures. She is the author of *The Expat Activity Book: 20 Personal Development Exercises for Gaining Insight and Maximizing Your Potential Wherever You Are*. Her articles and contributions have appeared in Global Living Magazine, *Raising Kids in the Foreign Service*, and on the Tiny Buddha website. She is also contributing blogger to I Am a Triangle. She loves to read, eat, run, meditate and have really deep conversations with friends from all over the world. Contact Jodi by emailing Jodi@worldtreecoaching.com or by visiting her website at www.worldtreecoaching.com.

Made in the USA
Las Vegas, NV
18 April 2024